RYA Foiling

© RYA
First published 2019
The Royal Yachting Association
RYA House, Ensign Way,
Hamble, Southampton,
Hampshire SO31 4YA

Tel: 02380 604 100
Web: www.rya.org.uk
Follow us on Twitter @RYAPublications or on YouTube

We welcome feedback on our publications at publications@rya.org.uk

You can check content updates for RYA publications at www.rya.org.uk/go/bookschangelog

ISBN 978-1-910017258
RYA Order Code G110

All rights reserved. No part of this publication may be reproduced, stored in a retrieval system, or transmitted, in any form or by any means, electronic, mechanical, photocopying, recording or otherwise, without prior permission in writing from the publishers.

A CIP record of this book is available from the British Library

Note: While all reasonable care has been taken in the preparation of this book, the publisher takes no responsibility for the use of the methods or products or contracts described in this book.

Co-written by Tris Best, Shaun Priestley, Sam Ross, and Amanda Van Santen
Cover design: Pete Galvin
Photographic credits: IMCA UK; Mark Jardine; Shaun Priestley;
Thorpe Bay Yacht Club; Paul Wyeth
Typesetting and design: Velveo Design
Proofreading: Matthew Gale

Contents

	Introduction	5
1	**Background Knowledge**	6
2	**Safety, Capsize Recovery, and Personal Clothing**	9
3	**Familiarisation: Windsurfing**	12
4	**Familiarisation: Sailing**	24
5	**Launching, Leaving, Returning, and Landing** – Windsurfing – Sailing	27
6	**Flying Safely: Sailing**	30
7	**Getting Started: First Flights** – Windsurfing – Sailing	32
8	**Sustained Flight** – Windsurfing – Sailing	36
9	**Understanding Righting Moment: Sailing**	42
10	**Manoeuvres** – Windsurfing – Sailing	44

Introduction

Hydrofoil vessels have been used on the water for many years. Motorised and sailing craft alike have adopted foils to decrease the level of drag in the water and increase the vessel's speed, range, and efficiency.

Foils have been adopted by development racing classes, offering an alternative performance range and providing a new sailing experience. Yet the scope for foiling is much greater, with manufacturers broadening horizons and introducing purpose-built foiling equipment for sailing disciplines such as windsurfing, dinghies, and multihulls, as well as both single and double handers. There are also retro-fitted foiling kits, which can be attached to existing equipment.

The foils designed for sailing and windsurfing differ slightly. The two most-popular foil types used on sailing craft are submerged T-foils and surface-piercing J-foils. In general, T-foils (such as those used on Moths) are more efficient and require a surface-sensing wand to control the ride height (the height of the boat or board above the surface of the water) actively. J-foils, such as those used on many catamaran classes and previous America's Cup classes, use passive height control, reducing lift as the boat flies higher. In windsurfing, the foil structure has evolved to enable flight and balance through one point of connection with the board, namely the fin box. While there has been some availability of windsurf foiling products on the market since the turn of the century, it is only since 2015 that the equipment has progressed sufficiently to bring windfoiling within reach of a confident blasting intermediate.

1 Background Knowledge

What is a Foil and how does it Work?

Knowledge and understanding of how a foil works will not only help in achieving initial flight success, but will also provide further clarity of how setup, conditions, and technique impact upon progression.

As mentioned previously, historically dinghies have used T-foils, and this will be the prominent foil type focused upon within this publication. A T-foil is made up of a vertical section with a horizontal wing attached below, replacing the conventional rudder and daggerboard. The main foil provides the most lift and also controls the ride height. The rear foil that replaces the conventional rudder is then used to stabilise the trim of the boat, just like the tail plane on an aircraft. Many boats are fitted with a twist-grip tiller, which enables the rudder trim to be adjusted on the fly.

In windsurfing, the foil is one piece, made up of a mast, fuselage, front (or main) wing, and tail (or stabiliser) wing, and simply fits to the hull of a board in place of a traditional fin. Just as in sailing, as the board gains speed and water flows over the foil's front wing, it develops lift, causing it to rise towards the water's surface, elevating the board and thereby reducing drag. The rear wing is also symmetrical and helps balance the foil by stabilising the fuselage in the horizontal plane, much like an aft rudder.

The size and shape of a foil's wing is carefully considered for each vessel. For example, the faster the vessel goes, the smaller a lifting area is required, creating the need to optimise the foil size for each boat type.

As the wing cuts cleanly through the water it deflects water flow downwards, exerting an upward force on the foil. This force creates higher pressure on the bottom of the foil and a reduced pressure on the top. The difference results in an upward force, lifting the foil and consequently the craft it is connected to. As the lifting force balances with the weight of the kit (be it sailing or windsurfing) and sailor, it will reach a point where the foil remains stable and the flight is sustainable. The amount of lift produced by the foil can then be determined by altering the angle of attack of the foil.

Angle of Attack

It's important to understand the angle of attack of a foil, as it clarifies how the lift force is created. The underwater 'wing' (which is our horizontal foil) has a leading edge and a trailing edge. The line in between the two is the chord line, similar to the chord line on a sail.

The angle the water flows over the foil in relation to the chord line is the angle of attack. By changing the angle of attack, the flow over the foil will create a smaller or larger pressure difference and therefore alter the lift created.

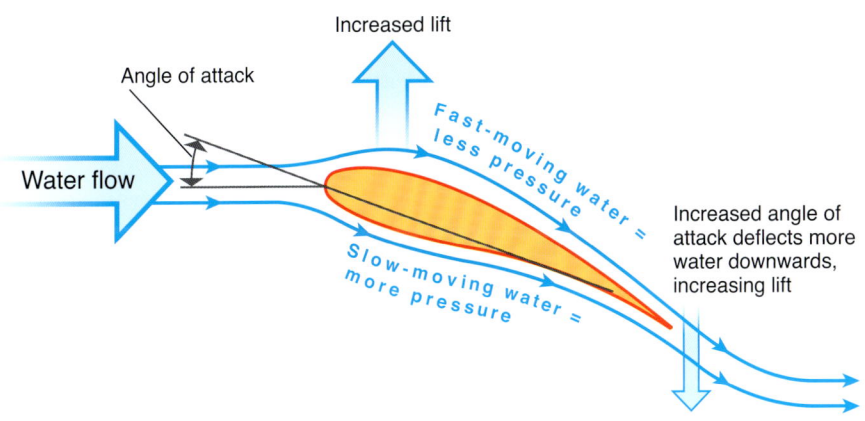

Apparent Wind

There are three angles of wind that we are interested in while sailing and windsurfing:

- True
- Induced
- Apparent

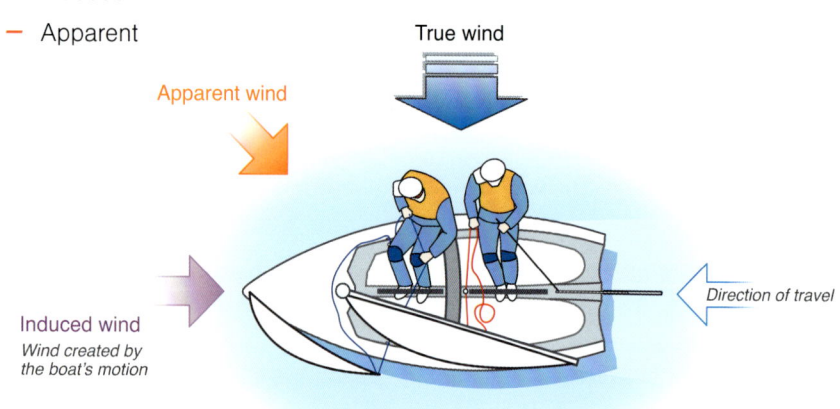

The true wind is the actual (or natural) wind, driven by the weather.

Induced wind is the wind created through forward motion. We all experience induced wind when moving forward, whether on land or on the water. As the travelling speed increases, the induced wind will also increase. For example, if there were no true wind, a cyclist would feel the induced wind as the wind in their face, or a 'head wind'. The faster they cycle, the stronger the head wind created.

Apparent wind is the wind experienced by a sailing craft when in motion. It's a combination of the actual wind (true wind) that blows over land and sea, and the wind created by their forward motion (induced).

Sailing vessels of all shapes and sizes use apparent wind. However, the importance of understanding apparent wind, and how it is utilised, is more fundamental for fast craft, and particularly in foiling. As a board or boat's speed increases and it starts to foil, it can reach speeds faster than the true-wind speed, requiring the sailor to trim the sail to the apparent wind. For example, if a vessel sails on an angle downwind at speeds above the true wind, the sail will start to back unless set to the apparent wind being experienced.

Due to the reduction in drag and the dramatically increased speeds of foiling craft, the need to adjust the sail (and boat angle for sailing) to the apparent wind is more critical than in slower craft.

Safety, Capsize Recovery, and Personal Clothing | 2

To ensure that a rider foils safely and has the best experience on the water, it is important for them to consider three factors – the environment, the equipment used, and their own experience and/or limitations.

Location, Conditions, and Water State

Launching and Landing

Water depth is a key consideration for both foiling boats and foiling windsurfers.

- Opt for lowering and setting up the foils before launching on specific winged boats (for example, on Moths you have to!), as they can be very unstable while trying to do this on the water.
- In windsurfing, with varying foil mast lengths now available, walk out to at least chest depth before turning the board over and starting the run. Similarly, landing in plenty of water should avoid any damage to the rider and their equipment.

Location and Weather

Flat water will make learning much easier as it will help reduce any variances in height during first flights.

- In sailing, due to the wand-height control systems in place, a steep wave can result in the wand tip losing contact with the water, reducing lift (or even generating negative lift!), and causing the boat's bow to crash into the next wave. In extreme instances (and especially on certain winged boats) this can result in the boat pitchpoling.
- When learning to foil, 11–16 knots (Force 4) is a good wind strength to start in. Experience and growth in awareness will allow a foiler to broaden the wind range and have a healthy appreciation for the limitations of both their ability and the equipment.
- Always ensure there is enough room to manoeuvre, and appreciate that the silence of flight brings with it an inherent risk of surprise. When foiling in close proximity to other water users, a rider will need to anticipate the manoeuvres of others who may not have heard them coming.

When on the foil, a boat or board's sailing angles are dramatically different to those of a boat or board sailing normally. The efficiency of the foil allows the rider to point higher or sail deeper, relative to the wind's direction, meaning it is imperative that they consider other craft around them. Knowing the equipment being used is also key. Different boats take off at different angles and learning to control ride height on certain points of sail is very boat-specific. For example, foiling-specific winged boats are easier to control while foiling upwind, whereas adapted boats will need to be sailed further off the wind to gain control. Once aware of this, a rider can determine their direction to control the power in the rig, the speed of the boat, and the height they are foiling.

Foiling acceleration and speed will be a whole new experience, and the silence of foiling will also make the speeds reached deceptive, so be prepared.

Proceed with Caution

Familiarise yourself with foiling. Take care around the foils themselves as their edges may well be sharp, particularly on the trailing edges. If damaged through misuse or grounding, the foils may not work correctly, creating control issues for either boat or board.

Foils need to be securely fitted. The lift increases the load placed through the equipment, increasing the need to ensure all fixtures and fittings are well located, secured, and maintained. Foils may move in their fittings, so it is wise to check all bolts and fixings again between sessions.

With windsurfing, rule number one of foiling, which should be adhered to in every instance, is '**Always keep hold of the boom**.' This should mean that any contact with the foil is avoided, regardless of the nature of the crash, while bringing the gear's motion to a halt. Until a windsurfer achieves a good understanding of where the foil is at all times, it is advised that they use uphauling rather than waterstarting to get themselves going.

Similar methods to righting a regular capsized dinghy can be used to recover a capsized foiling boat. Extra attention is required around the fragile foils (especially the sharper trailing edges), and on certain boats care must be taken not to put weight onto the edge of the vertical foil, where it attaches to the horizontal, as the vertical is prone to bending. It can be a struggle to climb back in, particularly on boats with wings. The sailor should aim to get back in the boat before it heels too far on top (to windward), thereby avoiding the boat capsizing again.

Personal Clothing

Appropriate clothing is best based on personal sailing level and the type of foiling participated in.

Conventional sailing clothing, such as most wetsuits, variations, and accessories, continues to be suitable for foiling.

When considering sailor level and the type of foiling boat or board being sailed (where capsizing or wipeouts are more likely if new to foiling), appropriate clothing is a must to ensure warmth and protection.

Impact clothing may also be a consideration, and is easily accessible, further reducing the chances of injury when stopping suddenly from high speeds. Although many foilers wear conventional gear, considering impact clothes may be worthwhile if you are new to foiling or intend to foil frequently on advanced equipment at speed.

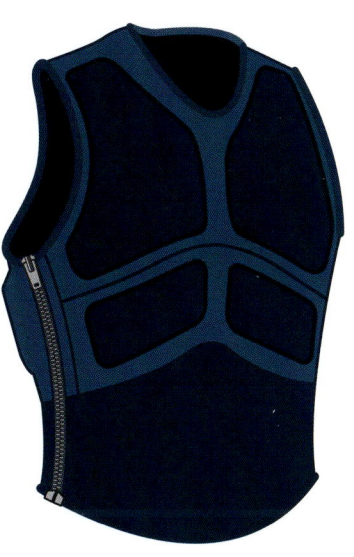

In the early stages of learning to foil, and when sailing 'standing-rigging boats' such as the Moth, wearing a helmet should be seriously considered due to sudden stops that can throw the sailor forward towards the rigging, mast, or boom. When windsurfing, or on boats that don't have much rigging, or boats with adaptive kits, helmets may still be prudent, but more reflective of conditions or personal preference.

3 Familiarisation: Windsurfing

The most common method used to connect a board with a foil is through a Deep Tuttle box head, making foils compatible with larger slalom boards, Formula boards, and some large freeride boards.

Advancements in design and development have seen the introduction of Powerbox converters, broadening the range of boards that can be used for foiling.

Base (or pedestal) plates are also used, ensuring the foil is located correctly while reducing the strain on the board's fin box. These also allow the foil to be moved forward and back, allowing tuning of the foil's position underneath the board.

Mast

Produced in either carbon or aluminium, the length of the mast varies greatly. The shortest masts available are close to 60cm, whereas the longest are around 110cm in length.

Mast Length

A shorter mast may well be beneficial while learning to foil, due to its lower riding position.

Shorter masts are also more compatible with narrower boards.

The limitations of short masts become apparent when travelling at faster speeds or through rougher water. In these instances, the wings are much more likely to break out of the water, creating control issues.

A longer mast is also more practical for use on wider boards, especially when looking to heel the board to windward.

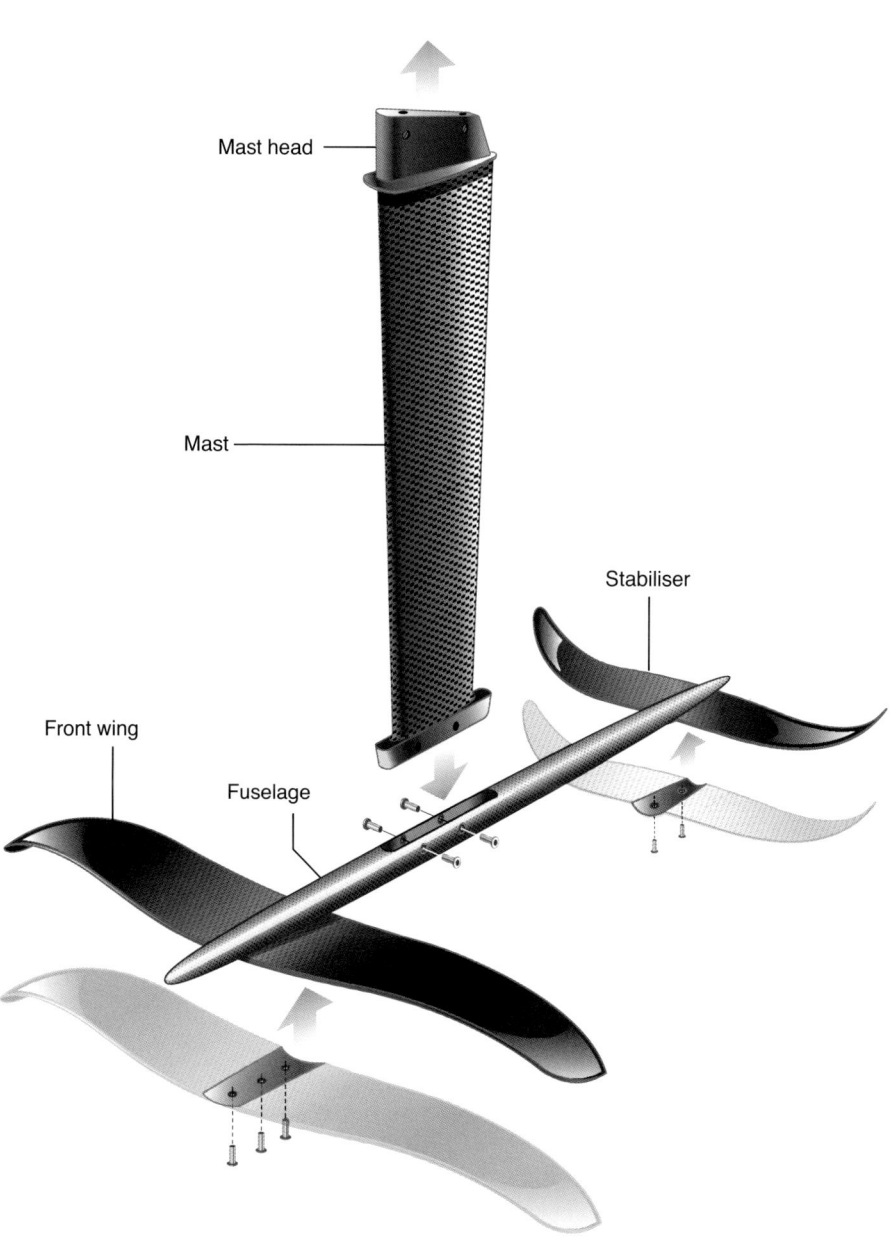

Fuselage

The fuselage of a windfoil varies in length, from 70cm–120cm, with longer lengths providing an improvement in ride stability, especially at speed. On most foils the fuselage can be dismounted from the mast for ease of transport and storage, while on several full-carbon setups the mast and fuselage are fused as one piece to maximise stiffness.

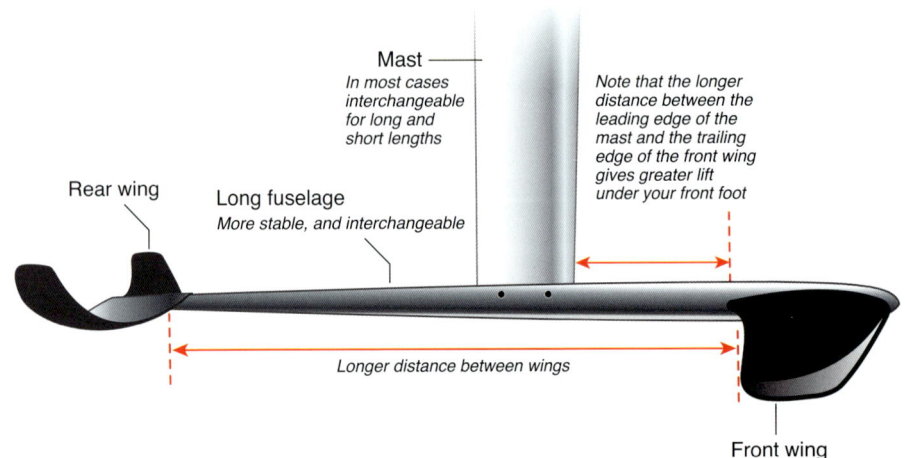

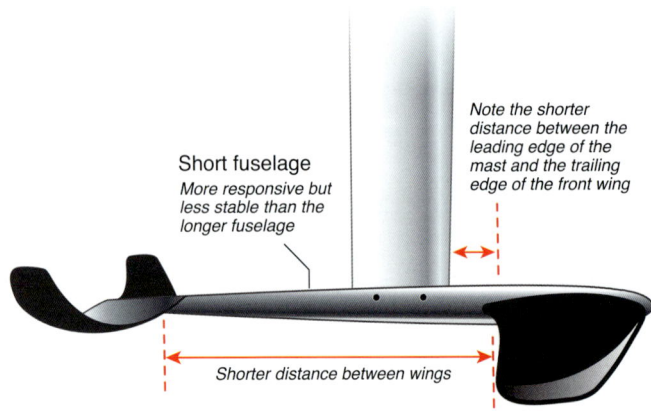

- The longer fuselage augments gybing stability, enhances ride stability and upwind/downwind performance.
- A shorter fuselage makes a foil more responsive and mitigates potential twitch issues.

Front Wing

The front wing is the main provider of lift. There are two main types of front wing:

- Low aspect: Often with the largest surface area, these offer maximum lift at lower speeds.

Front wing – LOW aspect

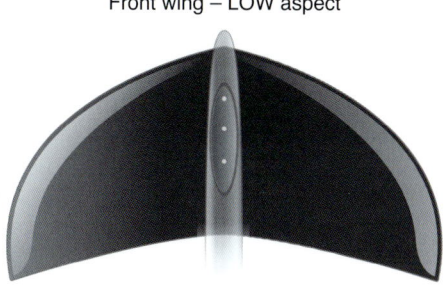

- High aspect: While still providing the option of large surface areas, these wings work best at speed and offer improved high-end performance.

Front wing – HIGH aspect

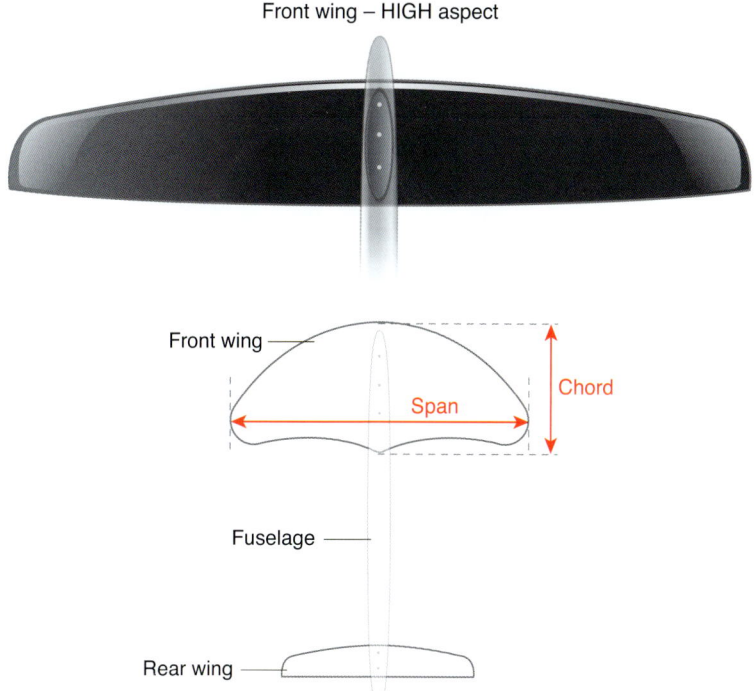

The front wing is often interchangeable to account for a sailor's ability, weight, or the conditions.

Rear/Stabiliser Wing

As with the front wing, the rear wing can be dismounted from the fuselage, although there is less focus on foil design and interchanging stabiliser wings as they have less impact upon lift.

- The rear wing can be tuned according to the performance you are aiming to achieve. For instance: a large front-wing-to-rear-wing ratio provides better upwind/downwind performance.
- A large rear-wing-to-front-wing ratio provides enhanced reaching performance and a more even setup for slalom.
- The angle of the stabiliser wing is tuneable on some foils, which increases lift and/or stability. A larger rear wing increases gybing stability.

Unlike many foiling boats, the sailor's body weight is used to maintain a level flight. The foil will not self-level and will need continuous input from the sailor.

Boards Overview

Fin Box

While foils will fit into any board with the correct fin-box type, there is a risk of failure if these have not been strengthened for foiling adaptation. Foil-specific and foil-ready boards have reinforced fin boxes to help deal with the loads of a foil.

Width

Board width is by far the most important parameter of a foil board, and should be considered in conjunction with the foil's mast length and the size of sail used to achieve the best setup.

A wider board should be chosen when using bigger rigs and longer masts to help maintain sailor distance from both the rig and foil.

More width provides more control over the foil's lift, with particular focus warranted by the width of the board's tail. A 70cm-wide conventional board is the narrowest that is really suitable for foiling. Some foil-specific boards are narrower overall, but will have substantially wider tails than their traditional counterparts.

To help illustrate this, consider a sailor with a quiver of wave sails no bigger than 5.7m. In this instance, the board selected could be narrower than 80cm, using a foil mast length of 75cm–85cm. A freeride sailor with maximum sail of 7.5m would require a board of at least 80cm to achieve the same level of control.

In order to push performance, the width of the board and the length of the foil's mast can be increased. The wider board allows the sailor to sail more powered while still maintaining control over the foil. It also allows the sailor to angle the board to windward in flight, achieving better upwind performance and more control in heavier seas.

The extreme of this is coupling a foil with Formula boards or Foil Race boards. These are up to 100cm wide and have very little reduction in tail width, which results in ultimate control and performance both upwind and downwind. The downside is that they aren't as suitable or comfortable for blasting across the wind.

Windsurfing: Foil Setup

Volume

Once airborne, the volume of the board has no real impact, but it does have a significant impact when getting going, especially in lighter winds.

When selecting a board size for any windsurfing discipline, the normal approach would be to consider the combined weight of rig and sailor (including water-wear), as well as sailor ability, the prevailing conditions, and the style of windsurfing intended.

As an example, a high-level intermediate windsurfer looking to blast in the footstraps on flat water would take their weight in kilograms, add 20–30 litres (L) for the weight of the equipment, and an extra 20L of reserve volume. The reserve volume provides the security to uphaul if required, and ensures the board is comfortable while non-planing, providing a good chance of releasing early when possible.

This is a good starting point for foiling as the sailor needs many of the same attributes from a foiling board. A board with 20–30L of reserve volume would be ideal for a foiler looking to go out in what might otherwise be considered light planing conditions.

If venturing out in winds lighter than this, though (i.e. hitherto deemed sub-planing conditions), the sailor could increase board volume to improve the chances of early flight. Reserve volume of 30–50L would not be uncommon, or even more if intended for use with large race sails.

If the intention is to windfoil solely in planing conditions, board volume can be reduced as it is in every other windsurfing discipline. Consideration must, however, be given to whether the reduced volume will necessitate the need to waterstart rather than uphaul – a manoeuvre with a new dimension where care must be taken not to kick the foil. When learning to windfoil, uphauling is therefore preferred, so a board with sufficient volume is required.

FOIL-SPECIFIC
Wide nose and tail shape providing more control over foil's lift. Rig size and foil mast length can be increased with a foil-specific board

CONVERTIBLE/HYBRID
Narrower nose and tail shape that can be used as a conventional board or for windfoiling

FOIL-READY
A conventional board shape with a reinforced fin box that can be used with a foil

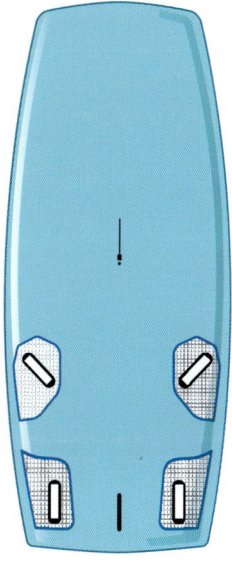
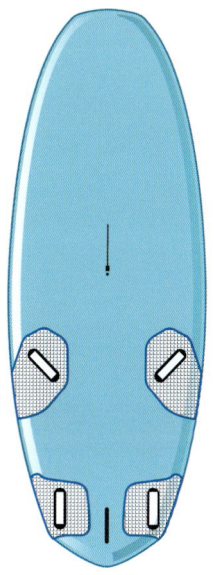

Note the wider tail and footstrap placement compared to hybrid and foil-ready boards

Mast Foot Position

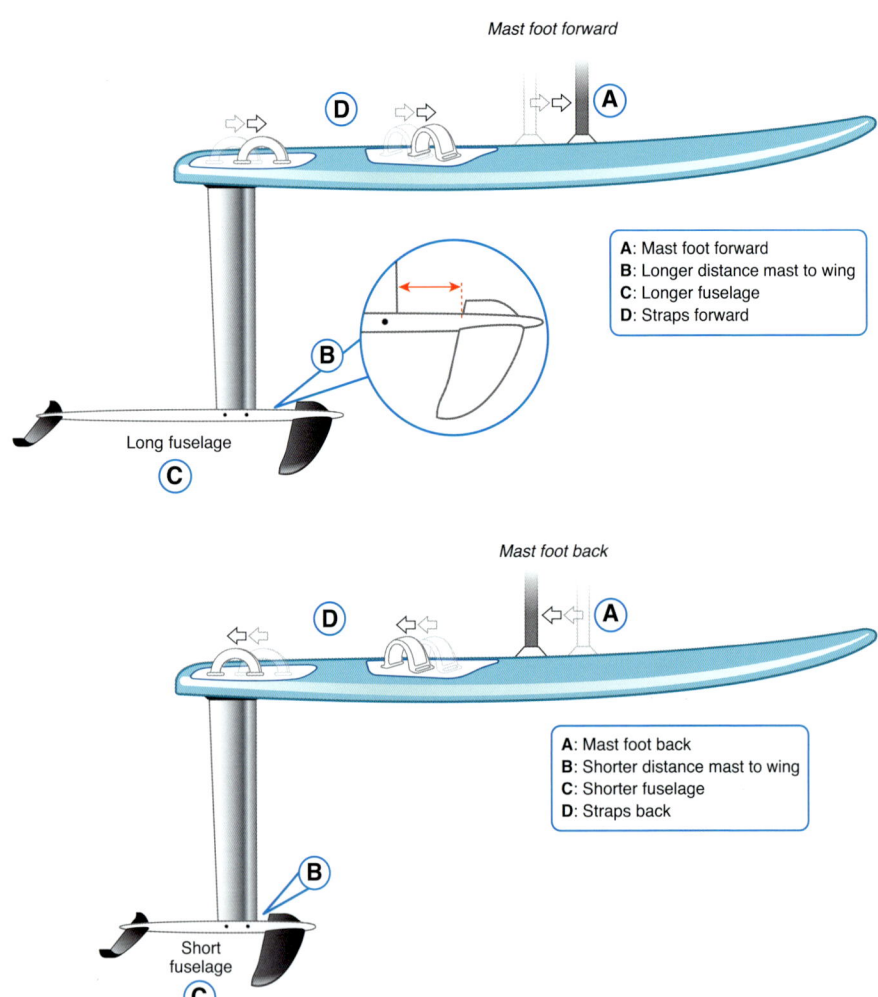

The mast foot needs to be set in relation to the lift of the foil.

Geometrically, the further forward the front wing is from the foil's mast, the further forward the mast foot will need to be placed in the board's track.

This can also be fine-tuned for subjective preference, moving the mast foot forward for less lift/more control, or moving the mast foot back for more lift/manoeuvrability.

Footstraps

The position of the footstraps relates directly to the location of the foil's lift. The general aim is to locate a sailor's weight over the centre of the lift generated by the front wing.

The larger the gap between the foil's mast and the front wing, the further forward the lift will be.

If this gap is small (under 10cm), the lift of the foil will be much more back-footed.

Forward-lifting foils should have straps forward, whereas rearward-lifting foils should have the straps placed back on the board. You could also tune this according to wind speed.

TOP TIPS

- Outboard straps increase control, especially if the board is narrow.
- To begin with, smaller straps will help with control, especially the back strap.
- When looking to gybe, increasing the size of the front strap will make carving on the foil much easier.
- A wide stance helps with trim control as it allows the sailor to shift their weight more efficiently from their front foot to their back foot.
- For more lift, move the straps and deck-plate back; for less lift move them forward.
- It's important to consider the position of the fin box in relation to the straps and mast-track when tuning the equipment setup. If the fin box is too far back it will be difficult to achieve the right balance.

A failure to fly or a lack of control during flight is most likely a symptom of poor setup, or poor foil/board compatibility.

Rig Type, Size, and Setup

In theory, any rig will work on a foil!

When first learning to windfoil, dependable power generated by the sail is incredibly helpful for achieving a first flight. In ideal wind conditions of between 10–16 knots, rigging a similar-size sail to that usually used (or only slightly smaller) will help to provide quick feedback and the desired lofty result.

As a sailor's foiling skill improves, the range of sail sizes that they are capable of using becomes wider. When competent and confident on a foil, the sail size chosen can be up to two sizes smaller than is otherwise used for conventional windsurfing. The windier it is, the wider this gap tends to be.

For example, in conventional 5.7m weather an experienced foiler could easily be comfortable on a 4.2m, especially if mostly reaching across the wind. In 7.5m weather, a 5.5m should be plenty for freeride windfoiling.

Increasing board width and altering their predominant points of sail will allow a sailor to manage bigger rigs comfortably. If sailing upwind and downwind, or searching for racing performance, a sailor could well be using the same-size rigs as they would in normal windsurfing.

Rigging correctly is key to getting sustained flight.

Rig Tuning

Due to the sail sizes used for foiling often being smaller than those normally used with such wide boards, there are some key rigging considerations:

- Less outhaul (i.e. neutral +/-1) is required, as the width of the board will often cause the rig to be over-sheeted. The extra draft in the sail will help to generate power in lighter winds and provide more dependable feedback.
- Initially (and particularly when using sails of 5.7m or larger), the rig can be set up with shorter harness lines as this will encourage the sailor to adopt a more upright stance when on the foil. As a rough idea, 22–28-inch adjustable lines are a good starting point.
- Ideal first-time rigs could be four-batten wave sails. Their softer profiles make them a little more pumpable, their draft breathing and expanding as pressure builds. Single or twin cams and multi-cam freerace sails (that are softer and more comfortable than full slalom rigs) offer excellent performance in light winds. Foil-specific sails offer many of these features, maximising the bottom-end power potential in minimal wind strengths.

Rig Options and Advantages

Sail Type	Pros	Cons
Four-batten wave sail	Light, powerful, and manoeuvrable. Good for control in first flights	Unstable at speed
Five-batten wave sail	Light, stable, and manoeuvrable. Good, as long as it's windy enough	Not as powerful in lighter winds
Freeride sail	Soft and pumpable. Stable at speed	May not hold shape or generate power as well through lulls
Single-/twin-cam sail	Good bottom-end power, stable, still light handling	Better if cams below boom and set on light mast
Three-cam sail	Good bottom end, still light, and able to pump. Ideal across a wide wind range	More technical sail to use
Slalom/race sail	Stable in high winds, fast, high performance	Less bottom-end potential, heavier and stiff for pumping

Advanced Tips on Rigging

Downhaul

The amount of downhaul applied can be reduced significantly for foiling, especially in marginal sub-planing conditions. The sail still needs to be able to rotate around the mast, but can have a tight, connected leech. As the conditions improve and the pressures in the sail build, downhaul becomes an increasingly important factor in determining the sail's shape and stability.

Foil-specific sails tend to rig with lesser downhaul loadings, and benefit from a softer rotation.

Outhaul

As with downhaul, the amount of outhaul applied can also be reduced. In lighter winds, an outhaul setting of neutral to positive 1cm–2cm should be used. When using small sails on wide boards, minimal outhaul should be employed to help prevent over-sheeting, therefore adding feedback and low-end power to the rig.

COACHING CORNER

- Not enough lift: Bigger rig or move everything back.
- Too much lift: Smaller rig or move footstraps/universal joint forward.
- Unstable flight: Move straps outboard or shorten lines and move boom up.

4 Familiarisation: Sailing

Equipment & Control Systems

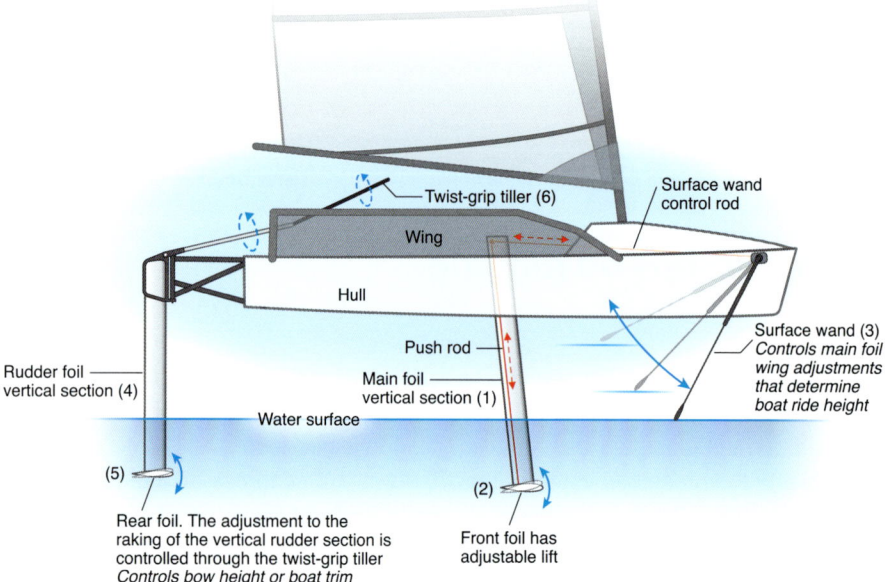

Foil and Boat Controls

Main Foil Vertical (1)

The vertical section of the main foil acts like a regular centreboard, providing lateral resistance. The push-rod system travels through the inside of the section, re-emerging at the base to connect with the horizontal section.

Main Foil Horizontal (2)

The push rods either articulate a flap on the trailing edge of the horizontal section (akin to an aircraft's ailerons), or the entire section itself.

From travelling up through the vertical section, the push-rod system connects to a bell crank at the top of the foil. In many foiling boats this is where the connection is made to the wand.

On adaptive kits, the system connecting the push rod to the wand is an internal system, with the wand attachment on the trailing edge of the vertical foil section.

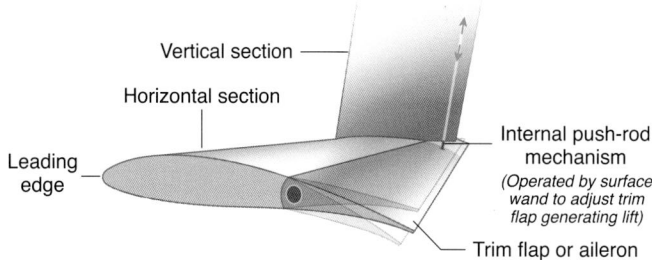

Wand (3)

Fitted to the boat's bow or main foil, the wand controls the lift generated by the main foil, altering how high the boat flies and enabling fine adjustments while sailing.

In foil-specific boats, the wand pivots from the bow (or a bowsprit), and through the push-rod system, directly influencing the angle of the main foil's horizontal section. The extent of lift generated can be controlled by the sailor using the ride-height control line on the 'barrel' – part of the system to connect the push rods from the wand to the main foil.

Rudder Foil (Vertical) (4)

The rudder foil (vertical) acts as a regular rudder, providing lateral resistance and steerage.

Rudder Foil (Horizontal) (5)

The rudder foil (horizontal) creates lift, raising the stern of the boat from the water and controlling its pitch and trim. By raking the entire rudder in its stock, the extent of lift through the rear of the boat can be increased or decreased, enabling the boat to be trimmed bow up or bow down.

Twist-Grip Tiller Extension (6)

A twist-grip tiller allows the sailor to rake the entire rudder in its stock, thereby altering the lift generated by the horizontal section of the rudder foil. As such, it enables the adjustment of the boat trim and bow height while sailing.

The neutral setting depends on the conditions, but the recommended starting point is to fly intentionally at an initially lower ride height, increasing to the desired setting once comfortable. This reduces the chances of flying too high, losing wand contact, or breaching. For the initial trim setting, the rudder should be fixed halfway, ensuring the boat is neither too bow up nor bow down.

Height Control

The main foil lifts the boat out of the water and directly affects how high the boat flies. Depending on boat type, adjustments to the amount of lift created (and therefore the ride height) can be made by altering the main foil itself. Without any height control the boat would simply continue to lift out of the water as speed increases, eventually resulting in crashing off the foils. The wand provides accurate and dynamic ride-height control automatically.

In boat designs that have the wand fitted to the bow, the lift created by the horizontal section of the foil is directly controlled by the wand's movement, which adjusts the flap on the section's trailing edge. A system of push rods in the boat and vertical foil section controls the lift created, increasing or decreasing the angle of attack on the main foil. Sailors can override the wand while foiling through fine adjustments varying the amount of lift generated by the foil, controlling the angle of attack and flight height.

On alternative designs (such as boats using adaptive kits) where no fine adjustment is available, tuning is carried out during rigging, engaging or fixing the main foil in place. A variance in the rake of the main foil increases or decreases the angle of attack, controlling the extent of lift and influencing how high the boat flies. This rudimentary tuning method is available on all foiling boats that have the option of securing the main foil in different positions.

Surface-piercing J-foils are used mainly on catamarans to comply with class rules. As the boat flies higher, part of the foil comes out of the water, as well as allowing the boat to slide sideways. Both actions reduce lift, which automatically controls the ride height, so no surface-sensing wand is required.

Launching, Leaving, Returning, and Landing 5

Windsurfing

Always keep the foil in front of you when carrying the board and foil together.

If possible, it is often best to assemble the foil and rig in the water, but you can carry the foil and rig together by holding the boom and using the foil's mast as leverage to lift the board up.

Make sure you walk out into deep-enough water, keeping hold of the foil at all times.

Once deep enough, turn the board over, submerging the foil in the water. It is best to uphaul to start, ensuring you stay well clear of the foil. Once sailing away, remember rule number one of foiling: ALWAYS keep hold of the boom! By adhering to this rule, you'll remain well clear of the foil in any subsequent crash or mishap.

Sailing

Leaving the Shore

As with all boats, it is good practice to carry out 'pre-launch checks' prior to launching, ensuring:

- the foils are correctly fitted and working
- the wand or trim system is working and correctly fitted
- foil attachments are correctly fitted and in working order
- the launch areas (both ashore and afloat) are checked and free of obstacles.

Some boats have foils that can be retracted, making launching and recovery relatively easy, whereas others have foils that require fitting from underneath the boat, necessitating the need to capsize the boat.

For boats with foils inserted from underneath, once you are at the water's edge with the mast across the wind, you can approach the boat from the stern, walk to the foot of the mast, and lift the boat into the water at its balance point. Once deep enough, right the boat through the dry-capsize method (avoiding weight on the foils) before sailing away.

Top Tip 1 — Know Your Kit

To ensure safe launching, it's very important to understand the correct setup for the boat being sailed. Many boats need to be capsized to install the foils, whereas boats such as the Moth can have their foils fitted ashore and be carried whole into the water.

Adapted boats need capsizing to install the foils. However, the foils can stay in the boat when using specifically made trolleys for the adapted versions. These trolleys enable the boats to be launched and foils lowered while afloat. Sufficient space is an important consideration to ensure the boat can be launched without risk to the sailor, the equipment, or other water users.

Top Tip 2 — Choose a Sailing Area with Plenty of Space

You need to right a capsized boat in order to get started after launching, or to lower and engage the foils so you are ready. It's very important you allow sufficient space to do this and take into account any leeway you may have when lowering the foils.

A benefit of adaptive kits is the ability to sail with the foils disengaged, assisting with launching and enabling you to sail to a clear area before engaging the foils.

With winged boats, it's safer and easier to have the boat set up before sailing, righting the boat in the water or climbing into the boat over the windward wing and not having to worry about engaging foils while sailing on an unstable platform. The sailor takes control of the mainsheet and tiller once in the boat, sitting on the windward wing, and trimming the mainsheet for balance.

Top Tip 3 — Pre-Flight Checks

Ashore: Check all pins are in place on the wings, and all pins for securing foils are ready. Ensure the tramps are tight and bladders inflated. Ensure the wand is in working condition and remember to untie the bottom of it before your first attempt at flying. For boats with adaptive kits, ensure that the centre-casing insert is secure and has no space to move back and forth. Check all the foil connections, from horizontal to vertical and from push rod to ball joint. Ensure the ride-height line is fastened correctly, with suitable tension around the barrel.

Returning to Shore

If possible, stop the boat near to a close reach, assisting the depowering of the rig and the ease of landing. Return to displacement-sailing mode with continuous awareness of water depth, stopping before running aground.

Neutral Settings

Having the ride height set correctly is the first key that will ensure the boat lifts out safely. Depending on the boat sailed and the conditions, adjustments to the foils may be required to ensure the boat is set up safely and efficiently. An awareness of the conditions is important but, if in doubt, start with medium ride height and medium lift on the rudder foil.

Capsize Recovery

The standard capsize-recovery method may be used to right a foiling boat. Be careful not to stand on the foils, and check that they are in full working order before righting the boat.

6 Flying Safely: Sailing

Initially, setting the foils up is focussed around trying to get the boat flying high enough so that the hull is clear of the water and the wand is working, but not so high that the wand loses contact with the water and the boat comes crashing down. You are also aiming to set the rudder foil to control the trim of the boat and ensure that it flies level (or slightly bow down as you improve).

Once the foils are set and the boat starts to lift, the boat speed will increase, followed by rapid acceleration. This is due to the boat's hull flying out of the water, reducing drag and enabling higher speeds.

Incorrect foil settings will mean they won't work efficiently, resulting in either insufficient lift to raise the boat out of the water, or lifting too high and coming back down with a bang! This latter issue tends to occur when the wand loses contact with the water. The foil tries to correct the issue by reducing lift and bringing the boat back down low enough for the wand to reattach to the surface of the water. In adaptive kits, the foil will level off to horizontal, ensuring the boat comes back down to the water-trimmed level.

On most foiling boats, the foil goes past horizontal and into negative lift, which very quickly brings the boat back down towards the surface, often into a nosedive – a situation increasingly apparent in wavy or choppy conditions.

Getting the correct balance to ensure the boat is flying high without the risk of the wand losing contact is very important in ensuring efficient performance. It rests primarily in controlling ride height, which is described in detail later.

COACHING CORNER

Ride Height

- More angle of attack on the main foil means more lift and more height out of the water.
- The push rod alters the angle of the foil. Depending on the design the push rod will either adjust the trailing-edge flap or move the entire horizontal-wing section.
- Adjust your main foil so you can fly the boat, but do not risk flying so high that the wand could lose contact with the water.
- Once you progress, look at trying to set up for the maximum possible ride height.

Pitch and Boat Trim

- Rudder-foil settings affect the pitch, and fore and aft boat trim.
- By increasing the lift of the rudder foil you are creating a force pushing the stern of the boat up, and therefore altering the trim of the boat.
- Set the rudder in a neutral setting for lift-off.
- Aim to trim the rudder angle to fly the boat level as you are learning.
- Look at trying to trim the boat slightly bow down as you improve.

Safe Settings

- Too much height can lead to the wand losing contact, resulting in a negative lift force being created on the foil, which drives the boat back towards the water. In wavy/choppy conditions, this can lead to nosedives.
- Retro-fitted foils have a system that doesn't allow for negative lift.
- If in doubt, the boat should be set with a low ride height and a neutral rudder setting. The ride height can be increased to the desired setting from here as the sailor's confidence grows.

7 Getting Started: First Flights

Windsurfing

Flying Fish

Aim

To hold short periods of flight time, touching down, and taking off.

Exercise

Initially, the sailor should try to blast along, pinning the board to the water by keeping weight forward and pulling down through the boom. The next exercise is to let the board take off, the sailor moving their weight back and releasing pressure from their front hand. Without getting carried away, they should then try to bring the board back down to the surface by shifting body and weight forward again.

This will give the sailor their first 'in-control' flights.

As they build confidence the sailor can extend flight time before moving on to 'sustained flights'.

Coaching Points

- Locking back heel down to keep the board flat.
- Moving weight back to promote lift.
- Hinging at the waist to maintain body position, reducing reliance on legs.
- Trimming flight height with front hand and feet.

What does Success Look Like?

Short periods of blasting with moments in flight, likely to be out of the harness.

Sailing

When not foiling, a neutral sailing position can be adopted by sitting towards the front of the windward wing, holding both the mainsheet and tiller extension, and maintaining a close reach with the sail eased. This will enable the sailor to rest in a comfortable position without using up energy. Continuously moving weight and position in and out of the boat to maintain balance is tiring and not necessarily efficient. It also often leads to capsizing, expending more energy swimming around and recovering the boat.

Once the foils are set effectively and with the boat moving forward, speed is required to generate flow over the foils, creating the lift for take-off. Sailing on a reach is encouraged, being the safest point of sail from which to take off.

The lighter, foiling-specific boats can also lift off on a close reach. However, this will require some accurate playing of the mainsheet to control your balance once up. So, aim initially for a beam reach and use the following practical techniques to take off:

- Balance (boat) – Place weight just opposite the mainsheet with the boat heeled to windward. It is key that the boat is heeled to windward – work to achieve this as the neutral balance point.
- Sail setting – Trim the sail to balance the boat with heel to windward. Work to keep the combination of a windward heel and an efficiently trimmed sail. Avoid over-sheeting, which is easy to do when trying to keep the boat heeled to windward.
- Trim – Moving weight aft can encourage take-off and is essential in boats using adaptive kits.
- Course – Once reaching, it may be necessary to make subtle steering movements to keep the boat powered up sufficiently and to control its balance. Try bearing away when overpowered and heading up when underpowered. The critical point here is that the steering is minimal.

Ride Height

The boat-control settings are able to manage the vertical lift created, controlling the distance the hull flies above the water. This is called 'ride height' and tends to be determined before leaving the shore through adjustment of the main foil's setting, controlling how much lift can be created.

On some boats, fine adjustments to the foils can also be made on the water, either in-board for the main foil, or through twisting the tiller for the rudder foil.

Novice foilers should adjust their setup to fly low and safe initially, increasing ride height as their skill and experience develops. Riding higher keeps the boat clearer of wave crests, provides more time during manoeuvres, and enables the boat to be heeled further to windward, gaining additional righting moment upwind.

On the downside, it is much easier to crash, as the lifting foil is closer to the water's surface. On purpose-built foiling dinghies, there is often a control line to help foilers adjust their ride height. Winding around 'the barrel' (a plastic fitting which allows the push-rod length to change), the control line enables sailors to alter how long the push rod from the wand can be and therefore controls the amount of work the push rod in the main foil is doing to adjust the angle of the horizontal main foil or main-foil flap. Through fine tuning of the control line and barrel, the angle of attack of the horizontal foil is adjusted.

On some foiling-specific boats there is the option to adjust the wand length. This also affects the boat's ride height as the longer the wand, the higher the boat flies.

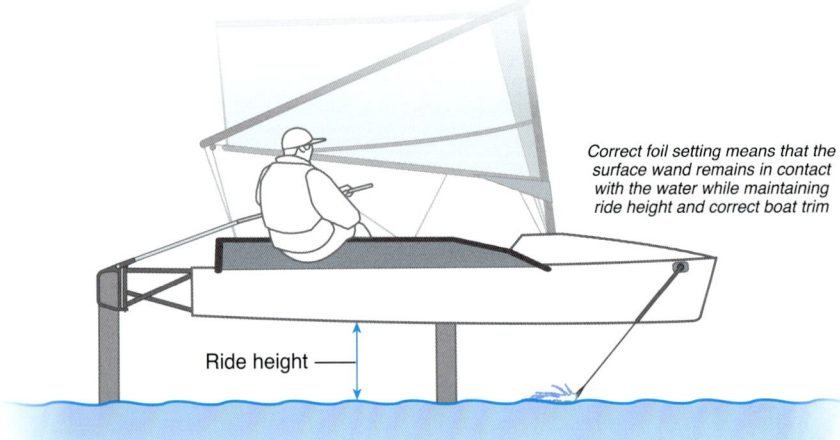

Correct foil setting means that the surface wand remains in contact with the water while maintaining ride height and correct boat trim

Pitch and Boat Trim

On many centreline foiling boats, the rudder foil creates lift by increasing the angle of attack on the horizontal section of the foil. This is controlled on many boats through a twist-grip tiller, which adjusts the overall rake of the rudder and, as a result, increases or decreases the angle of attack on the horizontal section under the back of the boat. The lift created from the rudder foil enables control of the boat's trim and adjustment of the bow up, level, or down. Other designs achieve this in different ways, and on adaptive kits a push rod changes the angle of the entire horizontal section of the rudder foil.

There is a link between the two foils and sailors can use this to their advantage. One example of this is that more lift on the rudder will trim the bow down, and therefore rake the main foil back, which results in less angle of attack on the main foil and so less lift and a lower ride height.

Most boats have a standard or neutral setup, providing a starting point from which to sail and initially get foiling. It is important, however, to understand that any change to these settings can greatly impact the control and performance of the boat, as well as any interaction between settings.

Principally, the rudder foil on all boats should be set in a neutral position (parallel to the waterline of the boat) to maintain the horizontal trim of the hull to the water's surface. It is then critical to adjust your foils to reduce lift as the boat flies higher, to maintain a level flight at your desired ride height.

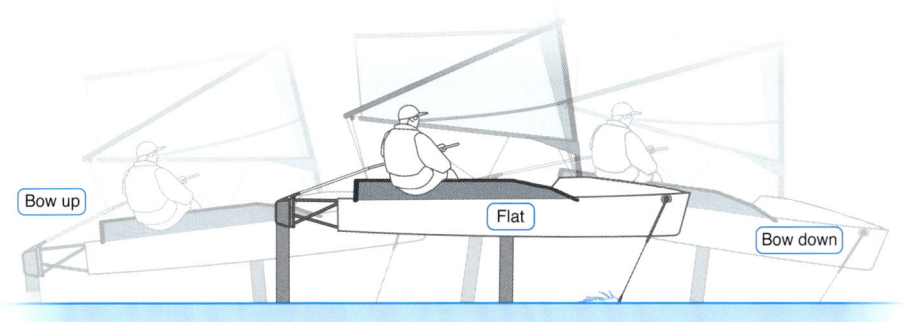

8 Sustained Flight

Windsurfing

Once past first flights, the sailor's stance can be developed to aid sustained flight.

Sustained Flight

Aim

Sustaining flight through a variety of conditions.

Coaching Points

- How to change foiling height through hand position and weight distribution.
- Starting to improve stance to facilitate hooking into the harness.

What does Success Look Like?

Short periods of flight with changes in ride height, and starting to get into the harness.

- ✓ Head: Looking upwind to spot gusts and lulls.
- ✓ Hands: Holding the rig still, front hand underhand grip, moving back and forward along the boom to manage height actively. Forward and pull down to come down. Back along the boom to increase lift.
- ✓ Hips: Kinked out to promote an upright stance and remain above the board. Hinge at the waist.
- ✓ Heels: Back heel locked down to trim the board and foil flat. Weight moving back and forward to manage height.
- ✓ Kit tweaks: As flight is sustained, boom height can be increased to help promote an upright stance.

Sign/ Symptom	Problem	Kit Setup	Coaching/ Solution
Falling to leeward	Not maintaining a flat board when foiling, most likely due to legs bending during take-off, or pulling on the boom while coming up	Footstraps too big	Focus on straighter legs and especially the back heel to control the trim of the board
		Board too narrow for wing or mast length	Lock arms or try underhand front hand
Spinning to windward	Too much lift through back foot	Front wing too big	Reduce lift by moving weight forward, or putting more pressure on front foot
		Mast foot too far back	
Extremely weighted back foot	Lift is too far back	Either adjust stabiliser wing angle, or move straps and mast foot back on board	Encourage sheeting rig in more when getting lift
Failing to foil	Not enough lift	Tuning of rig (may well be over-outhauled). Also, wing and rig size may be an issue	More weight needed on back foot
	Poor pumping technique		Increase board speed
Dropping out of harness lines	Hips and mid-line of body lifting	Shorten harness lines	Encourage hips to push out and maintain a straight back
		Raise boom height	
Can't maintain foil height	Not trimming for gusts	Reduce size of footstraps for more control	Begin by sliding front hand back and forward to help pull nose down
	Legs bending in gusts	Make sure rig isn't too flat	Also focus on the front foot helping to control height (fore and aft) and back foot control tilt, from rail to rail
Catapulting on landing	Lift too far forward	Move straps and mast foot forward	Make sure both feet are in straps when getting flight

Sailing

With the all-round foil setup correct, the boat should be ready to sustain flight. There are, however, a few key techniques to focus on at this crucial stage. As soon as the boat takes off, drag from the hull is reduced, leading to a sudden increase in speed. The acceleration, and silence, is spellbinding to the novice foiler! Due to this sudden surge in speed, the apparent wind moves forward very quickly, making it essential that the mainsheet is trimmed 'on' in time to complement the new wind direction. This will need to be done quickly and dynamically, and needs to be redressed constantly in order to maintain power and balance. Also crucial at this stage is the very subtle steering required to ensure that the boat remains heeled to windward. A bungee around the tiller can help prevent oversteering but, as there is now no hull to push through the water, the slightest tiller movement makes a big course alteration. The sailor has to make a conscious effort not to steer too much.

Once up and foiling, the sailor can now shift their body weight forward, controlling the boat's trim and placing the load over the main foil. The following practical techniques are required for sustaining flight:

- Course: Have a goal point (roughly across the wind) that you can use as a reference. Steer the boat to the desired course, re-trimming as required to maintain windward heel. Keep the boat under the rig and prevent heeling to leeward, which could ultimately result in capsizing.
- Balance (Boat): For best performance, the boat should be heeled slightly to windward. This provides additional lateral resistance from the foils, but more importantly increases your righting moment, enabling you to control the power and manage the balance of the boat.
- Sail setting: Once you have taken off, trim the sail for boat balance and sheet in, trimming to the apparent wind angle. Continuous trimming to maintain windward heel is needed to keep the boat balanced and on the foils. You can ease the sail to manage the power in the rig if you need to.
- Trim: If taking off on an adapted boat, move your weight forward as the boat sustains flight after take-off. This is to ensure you are not continually forcing more angle of attack in the main foil, which will lead to the boat leaping out of the water.

TOP TIPS

- Keep the boat heeling to windward as it has many advantages (see the Righting Moment section (on p.42) for further explanation). It ensures you increase your righting moment, which makes it easier to manage the power from the sail. It has benefits under the water as it provides more lateral resistance and provides a lift force, increasing your performance when sailing upwind.
- Be ready to sheet in and sail to the apparent wind. A foiler's apparent wind moves forward very quickly after take-off, as there is suddenly minimal drag through the water, leading to rapid acceleration. If this is not quickly countered by sheeting the sail to the correct angle, the sail luffs and the boat will start falling on top of the sailor, often resulting in a crash to windward.
- Ensure the boat is set up correctly for the conditions. It is essential to understand the basic functions and setup of the foiling boat. Without the correct setup, there is a risk the boat will lift too high out of the water, or will struggle to lift at all. Depending on the boat/setup, a sailor should always check their understanding of how the kit functions and how to make adjustments both on the water and ashore.

Fine Tuning

Depending on the conditions, a sailor will need to adjust the controls on their boat to ensure best performance. Often, the biggest adjustments needed are based on sea state rather than wind speed.

Ride Height

The higher a flight can be sustained the better, but, as the wind increases and the sea state builds, the risk of the wand losing contact with the water increases. This would result in the main foil (or main foil flap) setting itself into a level or negative lift angle, forcing the boat's bow down into the wave in front, leading to pitchpoles or sudden stops.

To mitigate against any chance of this occurring, a sailor should adjust their ride height, aiming to fly as high as possible while retaining the wand's contact with the water. On boats where fine adjustments are an option while sailing, changes may be necessary between points of sail (from an upwind to downwind course, for example). Due to the additional speed and the angle of the waves, it is often necessary to ride lower while sailing downwind.

Rudder Trim

After the boat is set up for the conditions, set the rudder for the most efficient boat trim, which is level or slightly bow down. The angle sailed to the wind is an important factor and changing the rudder setting as you change point of sail may be required.

When foiling downwind in windy conditions, reducing all rudder lift will keep the bow up.

Another top tip, which works well in boats with a twist-grip tiller, is to put maximum lift on the rudder foil in marginal foiling conditions, which ensures both foils are providing lift under the boat, increasing the chances of achieving flight.

Different Foil Options

Some boat designs offer the option to change the size of the main foil, and occasionally the rudder foil as well. To make the decision on which foil to use, the prevailing conditions must be considered. In general, the principle is to balance the lift/drag ratio, always aiming to opt for the foil that causes the least drag yet creates enough lift for the boat to fly.

On more-advanced foiling boats it is possible to change the foils completely, yet in the adapted/user-friendly foiling boats it may only be possible to change the tips of the foils, varying the overall wing areas.

Water temperature can also have an impact, as the increased density of cold water creates more lift, meaning that a sailor could choose a smaller foil than would otherwise be used in warmer water.

Sail Trim

Rig setup is boat specific, and referring to the rigging guide is essential. When learning to foil, mainsheet trim is critical, and to sustain flight, trim the sail to manage the power and drag as efficiently as possible.

Adapted boats may have different rig options, enabling foilers to get out across a wide wind range. In other specifically designed classes, it is important to achieve a flat sail to manage the power as the wind increases.

Light Winds

There is a big difference between low riding and foiling, as the speed increases dramatically once the boat lifts out of the water. The focus on sail trim is to get the boat flying – flat sails with twist encourage early flight, and usually the vang is the key control. Have the vang eased for take-off, but once foiling a sailor will achieve better performance by pulling on it and increasing lower leech tension.

Medium Winds

Once foiling, tuning the rig effectively will enable the boat to be heeled to windward at an early stage. Pulling on the sail controls such as the Cunningham and vang are essential in achieving this. On some specifically designed foilers such as the Moth, the vang has an important role in controlling lower leech tension and therefore pointing ability.

Strong Winds

In overpowered conditions, a sailor needs to do as much as possible to flatten the rig by increasing vang, Cunningham, and outhaul tension. Keeping their head out of the boat and being very disciplined with the mainsheet are also key.

Low Riding

Sailing efficiently in displacement mode is also important, especially in very light or heavy conditions where foiling is either not possible or unsafe. In light airs it is best to disengage the main foil, which greatly reduces the drag. In heavy conditions, retract the wand as far as possible and increase lift on the rudder to keep the boat in the water.

9 Understanding Righting Moment: Sailing

By understanding what righting moment is and how to use it effectively, a sailor's ability to achieve the best performance from a foiling boat will be enhanced.

Once a boat is up and foiling, balance is essential. If not corrected, any pressure from the rig heeling the boat to leeward will act as a force driving the boat back down into the water.

Leeward heel results in a decrease of lifting force, resulting in the boat coming off the foil and back into the water.

Windward heel enables easier boat management and control, with lifting forces in the sailor's favour, encouraging flight.

By increasing the righting moment, leeward heel and its impact on foil efficiency can be reduced.

The righting moment of a foiling dinghy is determined by the combined weight of the rig, hull, and sailor. The distance between this combined weight and the centre of lift from the foils is the righting arm. The righting moment will increase by either increasing the distance (heeling further to windward) or increasing the weight (hiking out further).

Once the boat lifts out of the water and is foiling, the centre of buoyancy (the hull) is replaced with the centre of lift (the foils) as the new pivot point.

As the boat is no longer in the water, the pivot point does not move as the boat heels, remaining as the centre of lift from the foils. This means that the more you heel the boat to windward, the more righting moment you have.

Relating this back to 'righting arm', in a foiling dinghy the righting arm:

- decreases as the boat heels to leeward
- increases as it heels to windward.

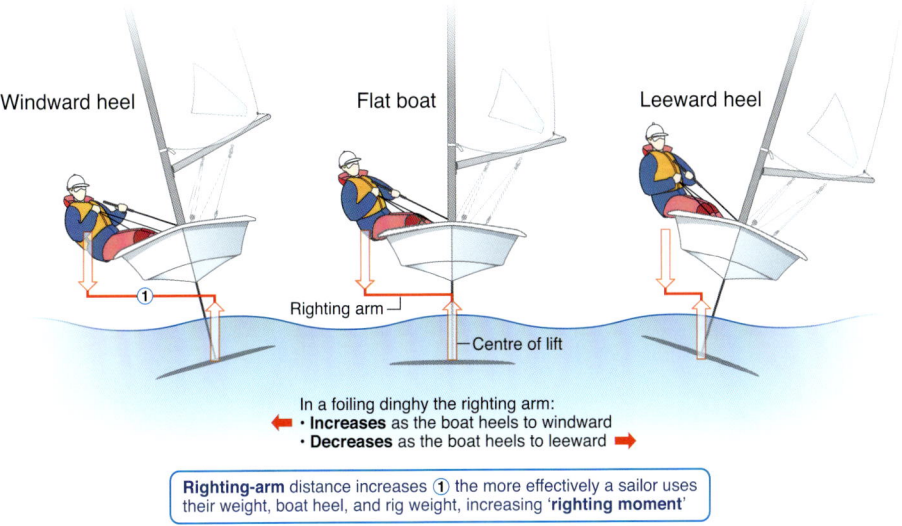

In a foiling dinghy the righting arm:
- **Increases** as the boat heels to windward
- **Decreases** as the boat heels to leeward

Righting-arm distance increases ① the more effectively a sailor uses their weight, boat heel, and rig weight, increasing **'righting moment'**

This is the opposite of a displacement dinghy and explains why the boat feels so different to sail on foils.

The centre of lift moves with the centreboard and the boat becomes unstable as it heels in either direction. You actively need to balance the forces to remain upright.

When foiling with windward heel, more lateral resistance is created. Windward heel also benefits from the lift from the foils, increasing lateral resistance and assisting progress upwind. Once a good technique is obtained and foilers are happy with upwind sailing, a further increase of upwind sailing performance can be gained through improved balance control. The more windward heel, the more upwind progress is made and therefore the less leeway. The diagram above shows the difference in lateral resistance under the boat.

10 Manoeuvres

Windsurfing

Tacking

① Preparation ② Entry ③ Midpoint 1 ③ Midpoint 2 ④ Exit

Once the sailor's weight is moved forward, the board will quickly drop off the foil, which means tacking can be completed easily on the water's surface.

A boom-to-boom transition reduces the number of hand movements and also helps to control height upon entry to the tack. Make sure your front hand is as close to the boom clamp as possible during the entry.

To try to foil further through the tack, a sailor's weight must be kept back as long as possible. The tack is similar to a carve tack, unhooking and carving into the wind. However, to maintain flight, the back foot stays in the strap as long as possible and the sail must be sheeted far over the board's centreline to maintain height past head-to-wind. Once through the wind the focus is on a fast transition, moving round the front of the mast, during which the board will drop off the foil.

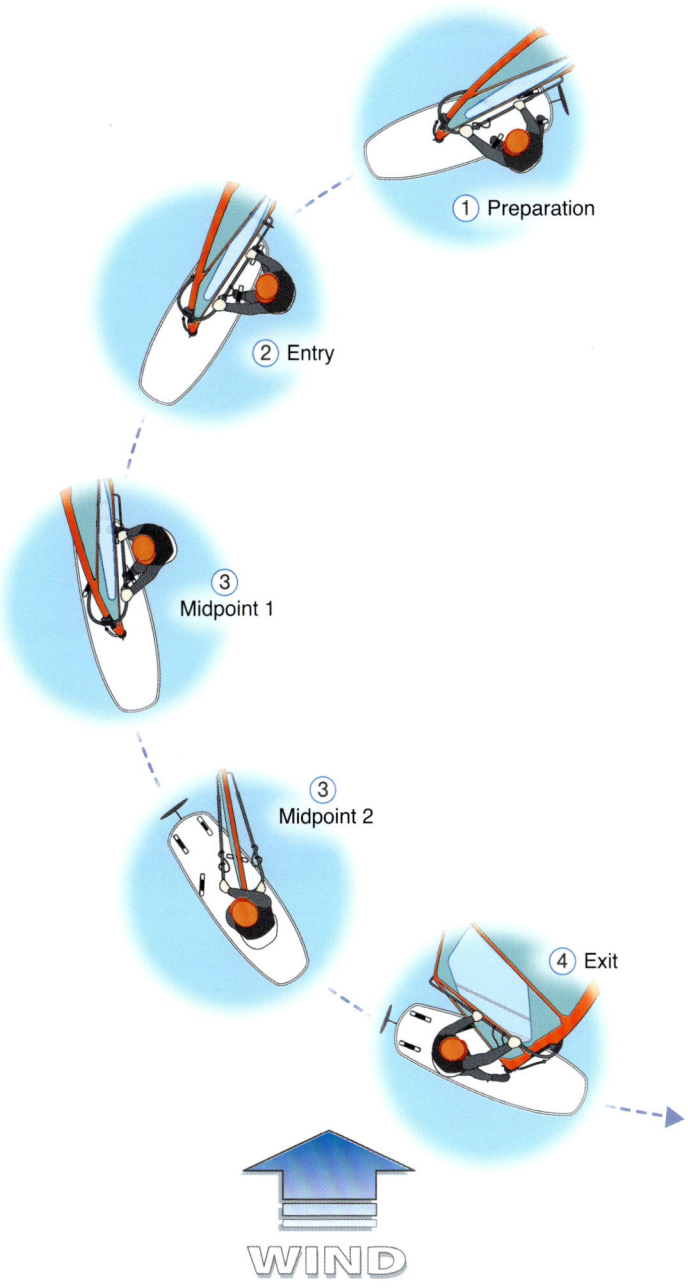

Once back in the straps and pushed off the wind, it is possible to elevate the board back onto the foil.

Gybing

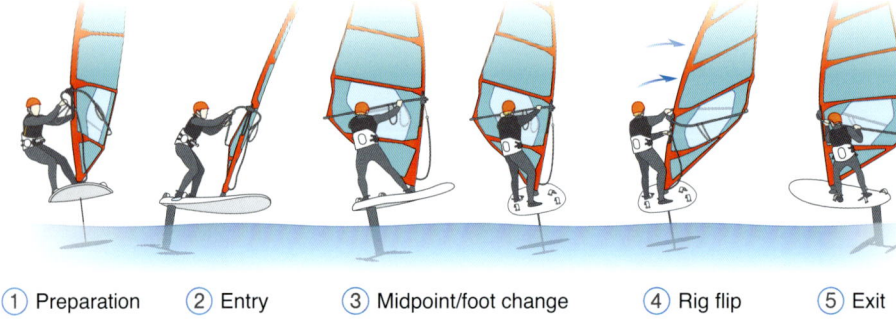

① Preparation   ② Entry   ③ Midpoint/foot change   ④ Rig flip   ⑤ Exit

When initially gybing, bring the board off the foil and gybe in a conventional manner. Keep the back foot forward to ensure the board stays on the water's surface, avoiding any unexpected take-off partway through the transition.

To develop the manoeuvre into a foiling gybe, the sailor must be able to sustain flight as well as sail off the wind with the back foot out of the strap. These techniques will provide the control and sailing angle required to foil into and (with practice) out of gybes.

To complete a successful foiling gybe, an intermediate sailor should already possess the required techniques; they just need to be identified, understood, and applied. The gybe is, in effect, similar to a light-wind or non-planing carve gybe.

The required technique comes with two challenges, the biggest being the foot change. The timing of the change is most similar to a conventional step gybe, although fractionally later. The main key to success, however, is placing the new front foot straight into the front strap on the new tack.

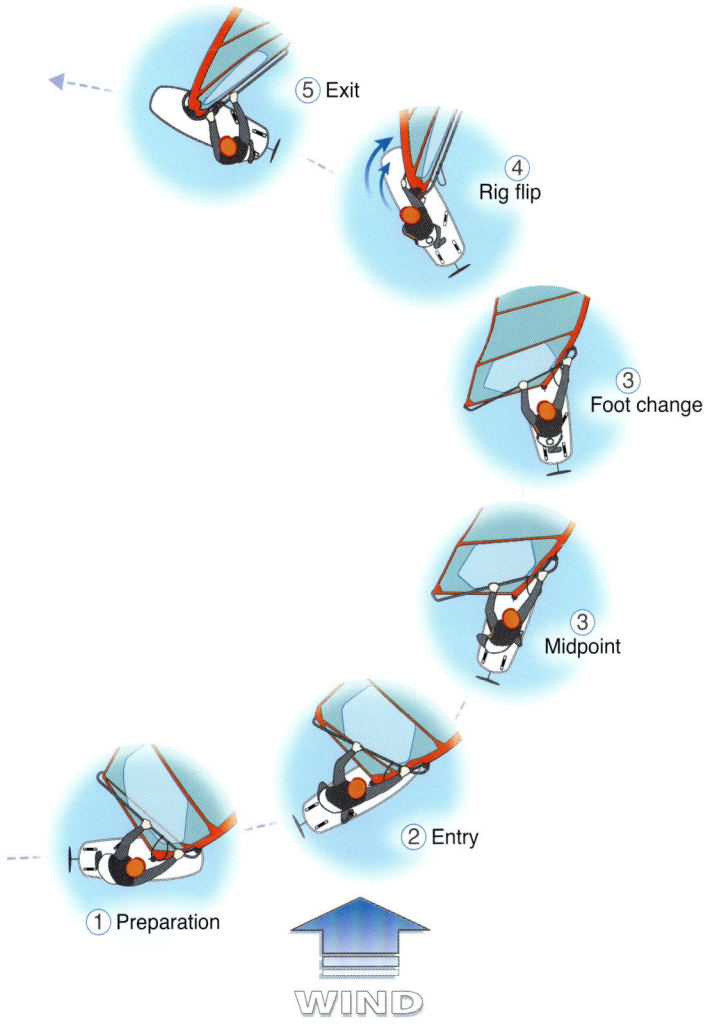

The second change is that during transition the rig needs to be upright, in the middle of the board. While it is still sheeted in (akin to a carve gybe), it is not laid down into the inside of the turn.

In windfoiling, a general trimming guideline is: the further forward our weight, the less lift we generate from the foil; the more rearward our weight, the more lift is produced. This is also true during the gybe.

Start by gybing on the water's surface, working on an upright rig and making a quick foiling foot change. Then slowly increase height upon entry until ultimately trying to do the gybe fully foiling.

Skill (and Session Considerations)	Teaching Points	Key Coaching Points
Gybing	Head	Look through turn
	Hands	Back hand down boom slightly, but sheet in so mast stays upright and forward
	Hips	Weight to the inside
		Weight forward to reduce height
		Weight back to increase height
	Feet	Back foot out to manage height in the middle of the board, then back foot across, just in front of back strap
	Foot Change	FAST!
		Front foot comes behind back foot, then new front foot goes straight into the new footstrap
	Ride Height	Start low to stop foil cavitation during the carve
		Also allows more margin for error during the gybe
		Height can be adjusted through weight transfer
	Timing	Set up, with the back foot coming out of its strap on a beam reach, starting the gybe itself on a broad reach. If powered, the deeper the entry. If less powered, enter on a reach
		Later foot change than for a normal carve gybe
		Similar timing to a non-planing carve gybe

Sailing

Tacking

In foiling, tacking is harder than gybing and takes many top-level sailors a while to master. It's only possible in certain boats and requires lots of boat speed on the entry, very accurate timing as the boat foils through the tack, and a low (sailing angle to the wind) exit. Training is certainly required but it is very good practice to try to keep foiling on the entry, and transfer your weight as the sail comes over. Even if you were not fast enough on the entry or didn't quite get the timing perfect, you are likely to complete the tack, coming out in displacement mode and preventing a capsize when you needed to turn round.

Gybing

Gybing on the foils requires very accurate technique and plenty of finesse to ensure a sailor can maintain flight while transferring their weight from one side/wing of the boat to the other. Key points are broken down below.

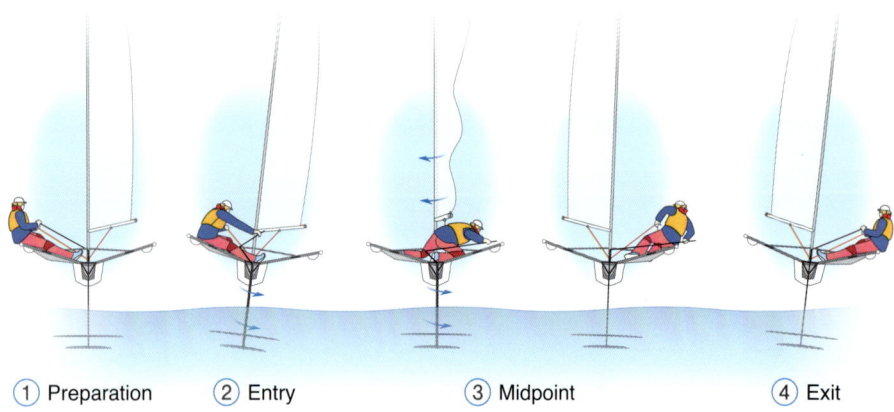

① Preparation   ② Entry   ③ Midpoint   ④ Exit

Ensuring the boat is set up correctly often requires a reduction in rudder lift, and/or adjusting ride height according to the conditions. Before attempting full-flight gybes, a sailor needs to be comfortable sailing downwind.

Entry

Slight leeward heel will help to carve through the gybe. Keeping the sheet in will ensure there is space to cross the boat and get under the boom to sail on the leeward side. The sailor must steer confidently as they move their weight inboard, but only using a small amount of tiller and/or rudder movements.

Midpoint

Stay low, keep sheeted in a little, and switch the tiller extension (either around the back of the boat or over the middle of the boat, depending on the design) before fixing the extension on the leeward side or wing of the boat. Securing the extension between the sailor's hand holding the extension and the wing bar will help prevent big tiller movements as the sailor moves their weight to the new side of the boat. The lighter the boat, the more opportunity there is for the sailor to take their time and 'glide downwind' while transferring weight.

Exit

The sailor should aim to get their weight out onto the wing, trimming the sheet for balance if required. The sail can be pumped during the exit, and hands switched once the boat is foiling efficiently on the new tack.

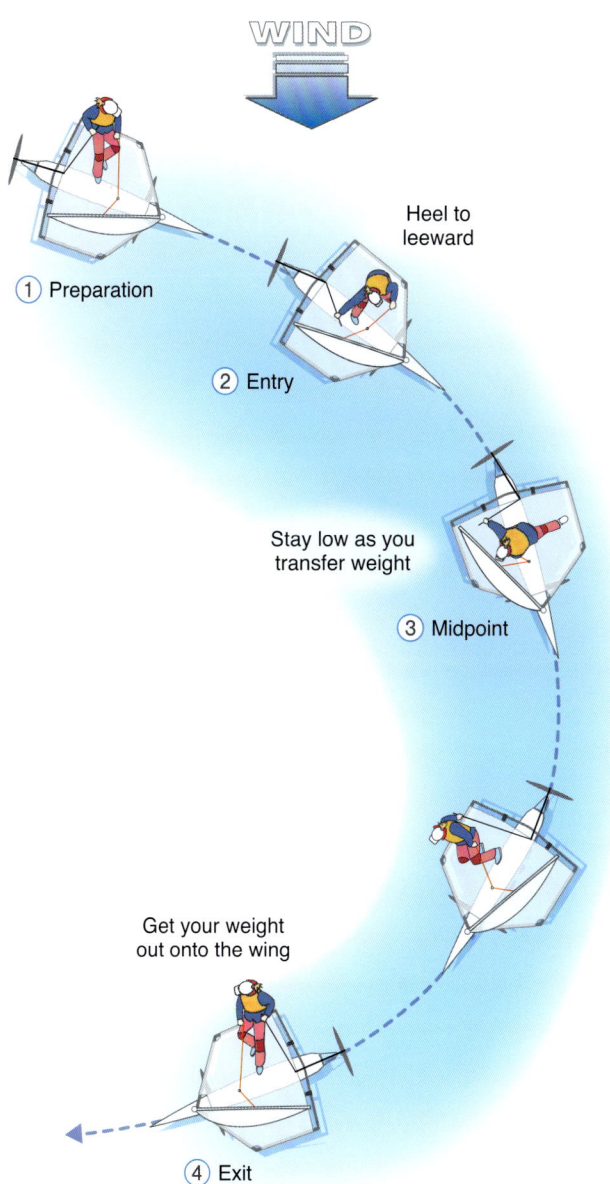

JOIN AND SAVE MONEY

WITH BENEFITS AND REWARDS DESIGNED EXCLUSIVELY FOR RYA MEMBERS

RYA Membership pays for itself with these great membership benefits and rewards:

- Free ticket to Southampton Boat Show
- Free worldwide third party windsurf and SUP insurance

- Great deals on clothing from marine brands
- Sail away with great offers and discounts on holidays

- Save on a new Volvo with the RYA Affinity Scheme
- Save on waterproof accessories and technical products

JOIN TODAY at www.rya.org.uk/go/join